Neighborhood Animals

by Riley Brooks

PEARSON

Scott
Foresman

Editorial Offices: Glenview, Illinois • Parsippany, New Jersey • New York, New York
Sales Offices: Boston, Massachusetts • Duluth, Georgia • Glenview, Illinois
Coppell, Texas • Sacramento, California • Mesa, Arizona

Photographs

Every effort has been made to secure permission and provide appropriate credit for photographic material. The publisher deeply regrets any omission and pledges to correct errors called to its attention in subsequent editions.

Unless otherwise acknowledged, all photographs are the property of Pearson Education, Inc.

Photo locators denoted as follows: Top (T), Center (C), Bottom (B), Left (L), Right (R), Background (Bkgd)

Cover ©levranii/Fotolia; **1** Getty Images; **3** Micha Fleuren/Shutterstock; **4** ©Royalty-Free/Corbis; **5** Getty Images; **6** Alex oo1/Fotolia; **7** ©levranii/Fotolia; **8** teekaygee/Shutterstock.

ISBN: 0-328-26355-9

Here is a bird.

Here is a squirrel.

Here is a butterfly.

Here is a bee.

Here is a rabbit.

Here is a snake.